WHERE THE DEAD POETS SING

WHERE THE DEAD POETS SING

poems by

MICHAEL CURRAN-DORSANO

WAYFARER BOOKS
SAN JUAN MOUNTAINS, COLORADO

WAYFARER BOOKS
SAN JUAN MOUNTAINS, COLORADO

All Rights Reserved
First Edition Published in 2026 by Wayfarer Books
Cover Design and Interior Design by Connor Wolfe
Cover Image © Manus Walsh
TRADE PAPERBACK 978-1-965320-62-4

10 9 8 7 6 5 4 3 2 1

WHOLESALE INQUIRIES? You can find our books available via Ingram, offered with standard trade terms and lifetime returnability. With printing bases in the US, the EU, the UK, and Australia, Wayfarer has the capability to fulfill orders globally. Our titles are available wherever books are sold in paperback, ebook, and audiobook. Find our books at local Indies, Bookshop.org, iTunes, Barnes & Noble, Amazon > US & International, or direct at wayfarerbookstore.com.

WAYFARERBOOKS.ORG
WAYFARERMAGAZINE.COM
WAYFARERBOOKSTORE.COM

SUPPORTING INDIGENOUS FUTURES
1ˣ GIVEN BACK

To all the friends, family, and strangers
who gave me shelter from the storms.
And a special thanks to Manus Walsh,
for his brilliant painting, and Féilim James
for editorial and translation.

TABLE OF CONTENTS

INVOCATION

Old songs dwell in me
like river stones,
smooth and still,
sunken deep in cold dark sleeping,
their meaning locked away
in rock and mud and creeping moss.

They lay unseen
'neath the shifting reeds,
the roaring rivers and willow trees,
lost and buried
'neath the rushing tide
of days and months and years gone by.

Forgotten by the winds,
the rains and skies,
tumbling clouds and lovers' sighs,
silent songs shaped
by soft hushed cries,
by keening souls
now petrified.

CASANN AN ROTH

Beyond the edge of reason from starboard to port the sailor sees
dream walk on dream the feverish memory of birdsong through the
cycling seasons swallowed by the sea of autumn leaves that once
crunched beneath his tiny feet floating free on the ocean breeze
with waves curling steam cresting from the puttering engine to kiss
that sacred line between darkness and light rising to join the long
sleepless night as root and branch hewn and bound to form his
bobbing ship drone with the sounds of the forest floor torn from
fresh flowing streams now carven husks that gleam with names of
those he left behind in the sunken caverns of his flickering eyes their
wick charred and yearning for the dark awaits the stern the wheel
of his ancestors turns again his fate their fate he knows now as the
sailor plows through the unkempt braids of foam and brine of a
strange new goddess

SONG OF NO BEGINNINGS

The father looked just like you,
same roving mustache and beatnik hair
dew drops glimmer, in their reflection a shimmer
of the neighbor's kitchen laid bare,
all the years and years
of renovations yet to be done,
our 'for sale' sign hung only days ago,
nestled now in the vined trellises.
I don't think I'll ever come back, my mother lilts,
knitting a tight-fitting cap, a parting gift
for the young boy who sits in bliss peering
through wrought iron and juniper wondering
if summer does indeed ever end.

I feel I've already left,
the road rising to meet each step
on this crumbling path of tiled clues
my father and grandfather laid, weaving
through the Bleeding Hearts my mother sewed;
their blossoming memory owed to her mother's hands,
perhaps an ode to this distant land,
urging me on in the passing song a stranger hums,
the notes old as the beat of the bodhrán drum,
that booms now in the creaking rafters,
boat wind-worn and battered,
this new chapter of chapters ending as it began:
the promise of new life on foreign sands.

SHIPWRECKED

chiseled to bits and bobbles left to drift like flotsam on the tide of
history repeats on repeat can't sleep soiled sheets no heat just dark
matter at the center the event horizon bending me closer and closer
to your weight in my arms you small careful reckless thing needs to
be confused abused and forgotten to exist let me kiss forgiveness like
a blanket for this sacred cow light bringer day slinger face changer
bleating sheep eat me digest me mold me unmake me consecrate
this bliss

Touch me. Prove that I exist.

LOCKDOWN

I never thought I'd see, they'll say, the pubs closed down on Paddy's Day, the pasta shelves in Italy, picked and stripped and bartered empty, the President of The United States shake infected hands with the human race, I never thought I'd see the day, I never thought I'd see, they'll say I never thought I never thought I never I, I never why I never knew I used to then but now what now where to and you and you and you and I they'll say, there still must be a way there still must be there still must please no empty shelves no empty shells no empty streets no dead dreams that sleep in headlines that creep through pubs and presidents to screens, no resonance the frequency is garbled now, the channel is stuck on

INTERLUDES

It's okay to escape sometimes, she said
Everyone needs a break, she said
Sometimes the lies we make, she said
are the ones that save us in the end.

I was chasing seals the other day,
up and down Galway Bay
but I fell,
so I spent the rest of the day
face down in the sand,
seashell in hand,
listening instead
to what the waves had to say,
as they splashed up and down
Galway Bay.

SALTHILL

His thoughts stretch
across wet stones,
Is this home? He asks,
Is this at last where I'm laid to rest?
Seawater laps his craggy nest
of moss and rock and seaweed,
West, lie the bones of his ancestors,
the ones who left, *is this home?*
he asks, with each splashing caress,
his thoughts contract,
unspool, undress,
down to the waves of his rasping breath
waking her name,
in his sunken chest,
yearning to rise, and singing
crests *Is this home?* he asks,
Is this home?

WEAVER AND WANDERER

In the shadows that cannot speak,
        between this world and dreamscape,
where soul meets itself again and again,
        a continuum of sacred symbols warp and bend
the black light of time interrupted,
        to kaleidoscopic threads that spread
through every woman I meet, in their eyes
        some piece of you speaks.
Each thread ends where paper meets pen, each stroke
        spooling us closer and closer together,
from inky tatters to patchwork cloak,
        when we last spoke I knew
I could never escape the tapestry of you,
        your design certain as rain-swept shores,
sun-washed stone, the trembling tones of guitars
        that wander me down Quay Street.
Knowing these steps of no direction,
        along these paths of aimless connection
carry me step by step by sacred thread
        to you, I walk in silence
between this world and dreamscape
        so shadows may one day speak
in time, again, complete.

ROSMUC

Winding up the stone-walled lane
past bramble, hawthorn and heather we came
to a fence swung wide, all the signs pointing
to a bull inside, but struck more
by the silence
borne in the corroded walls of your home,
ancient stone abandoned a century ago,
fleeing this teanga Ghallda you'd never know,
with only the forbidden salt-wind syllables
of Connacht—the Gaeltacht they call it—
blood of your blood ever strangers in speech.
Perhaps you could only
ever speak to your children in touch
or on wordless waves of thought.
And perhaps in knowing
the bramble, hawthorn and heather,
these sea-song secrets,
I'll know you better as my mother stands
resolute, lost amongst the vines and shoots
that entomb these memories of you.

SONG OF SAND AND STONE

Each day with you
was a hundred years of gentle waves
splashing tears upon stony shores,
barren and coarse,
drawn from the depths of the ocean floor,
every droplet
changing the shape of me,
with the burning salts of the raging sea
you carved your name
in my moss-covered cliffs,
painted my caves with hieroglyphs
of sand and sea and ocean air.

When the tide pulled out
and you left me bare and dry,
if stones could speak
you'd have heard them sigh
for the day that the tide
comes rushing back.

A TIP OF THE CAP

Ancient but not old, no
voice trembling but proud, yes
walks on four legs but never begs,
stands tall and shaking,
cape and weathered cloak
shrouding his withered frame,
reciting again and again
an ode to his Dear Boy,
oh not his son, but a stranger,
an actor no less,
whose Irish name I couldn't even guess
if I tried, dead now,
but the old man doesn't cry, no
with eyes unwavering he lilts
Dear Boy, Dear Boy, Dear Boy
bringing him back to life
for a short time, another encore,
a tip of the cap,
or to rehash that moving metaphor
that brought the old man
to question to ponder to rethink something
he thought he never knew,

Dear Boy, he says again
but the subtext, the clue plucked
from beyond the final curtain

Remember me?

      Remember me?

Remember me?

      Remember me.

SONG FOR THE UNDYING

He sits in wait amongst the dead,
draped atop
his obsidian throne,
his eyes, hollows
of bioluminescent spring,
sworn to bleached fingers
his sparkling cyan rings pierce
the halls of the undying,
his legions silent,
in suspended animation,
the echoing tap of his knobbed
knuckles clacking,
drumming his warriors to sleep.

Oh what dreams may come
to the waking world,
when the dead King's rappings cease?

THE OLD GODS

oceanic currents changing direction pulling back to crash against the
shores of their creators their point of convergence the energy of our
choices individual collective past present future colliding gale force
winds riding the needle of the Doom's Day Clock to the threshold
of midnight a synthesis of our near-sight all the buying the selling
the lies we keep telling to escape with the herd that keeps trucking
on to the sweet song of our shepherd singing distraction reaction
fear hatred for centuries we've cut drained burnt and pillaged
remoulded the Earth in our vacant image now life pushing back
with a pandemic a global market collapse and storms bearing down
on Galway night after night unlike anything this island nation has
seen as grocery stores are picked clean borders shuttered and those
words uttered again and again *I've never seen anything like this before*
now we must return to clay and reform this violent ever-changing
world to the Old Gods of wind and rain and sky and branch of
earth and flame they sing again their ancient refrain and we apes we
wild selfish apes must pray it is not too late it's time to run so run
monkey run

ASCENSION

Time out of times
the shag fool climbs,
pincers grasping for signs
of sandstone grooves
to grip, a slip, he moves,
his paws searching for serenity
in the halls of the harrowing winds,
bellowing the cliff's chanter,
its drones clip-clop canter
the triplet banter of wind-song,
diving beneath to seas
of forever falling,
ever ascending he prays
for the old ways of dreamings past
to pass at last
through burning skies
and star-fall.

Canção para a Amazônia

In this arachnid embrace,
weaving the threads of the dead
round my waist, milk-white rivers of fate
spider up your sacred valley, cursed
with your exodus
to this teetering precipice where
the wails of your ancestors echo,
gnashing saw blades
 desecrate grove and temple,
the drums of naked feet on the earth,
pounding for rebirth shivers up my spine
as I patiently climb to the well of your neck,
its soft honey glow beckoning me
to slow, finally to slow and spread
my fingers along the edge of the bed,
press my chest against yours as tears pour
apple blossom and sun ray remembrance,
every bruise, fresh torn skin,
burning with the distant cries of your kin,
as we rapture blister untwist can't resist her,
what god clipped your wings you uncharted thing,
what god dared clip your wings?

DREAMS OF A DYING EARTH

I've seen these days before, these long, grim, uncertain days, I've seen them play out before me in waking dreams of fallow fields, littered with shells of giant harvest wheels that turn no crop, rotten homes, gutted shops, clouds bellied with soot and ash engulfing sun, the masked children run untouched, unseen through empty streets, these days that tumble into weeks, no relief in sight, visit me now like a death rattle, black breath from the cradle, where shadowed fingers spin threads of time and space, in dreaming remembrance of our human race, into the fraying tapestry of one Earth, one Fate, too late, too late, once more, once more, I've seen these days before.

I CAN'T BREATHE

silent screams blaring on every frequency beaming from a thousand
satellite feeds the video plays 9 minutes 29 seconds can't look away
from this day of days we all knew would come nowhere to run
from the masked men unmarked vans and guns the voiceless stand
mute while rubber bullets shoot through soiled air can't bear the
weight of picture after picture of smoke blood the fissures running
deep beneath cracking concrete blister and burn street after street
black brown white feet marching to the hoof beat of native drums
pounding sounding their ancient sorrow seeded in rotting dirt of
this land that gave birth to battering rams shattering blue shields
guarding the twisted heart of a nation cursed from the start of an
insurrection an infection of only one complexion conspiring to
overthrow an election their code repeating repeating buried deep
in the operating system seeping from their pores a virus older than
mine or yours on waves of static to this attic asymptomatic but body
still convulsing the cries of friends family pulsing through me losing
more and more light to the long sleepless night sinking closer and
closer to

мир (peace)

Twas a quiet day,
on the cusp of May,
when, at last, the sun arrived
on wingless winds,
on pebbled skies,
on the clouds hung round her eyes.

Across Galway Bay,
she gazed far away
to where storms rumbled and bled
with thrumming steel,
with blazing lead,
with the silence of the dead.

But a hundred strong,
her kin marched along,
past rows of pastries and tea,
their wordless cries,
their blackened seas,
their families sang out to me.

The villagers came,
swearing off the rain,
for a laugh, some craic, and they
with weightless words,
with smiles, prayed
for peace at the break of day.

Down the Burren way,
her gaze seemed to say,
"Perhaps at the cusp of June,
when the storms have passed,
I'll return at last.
May I hold my husband soon."

ONLY TIDES

In memory of Liam Burke

From He to It,
Is to Was, There to Where
have you gone my dear friend?
Wandering wondering as you always did?
Or have you found that peace at last
that you never could quite grasp
in this sleepless dream,
waking sleep,
of life and death,
of sky and earth,
this delicate bundle of matter
bound together under gravity's finger,
the pressure snuffing your brilliant embers
of whimsy, wit and swagger?

Your body a dagger,
Osiris obsidian midnight sun shattered,
eclipsed beyond the dancing curtains,
veiling our mortal unknowing,
heartbeat slowing as I kiss
your frozen crown, your tweeded majesty,
you wizard, king, lover, friend,
eternal player strutting the stage
again and again I will miss you,
as your aching spirit passes I kiss you,

now wondering wandering
from when to then,
him to grim knowing that here
is what I fear,
that there is nowhere left to hide
on the other side of that fluttering silk lies
only tides,
only tides,
that cannot be grasped, felt, fucked,
seen, heard or killed,
cauldron of damnation, redemption,
absolution and suspension to I hope
ascension perhaps dispersion I pray
rebirthing for why
would such a light be held from waking,
unless some lonely god longed to kiss
your flaming brow, naked majesty,
caress your sprightly spirit,
so it might remember,
in its dismembered silence and shadow
what it meant to be alive.

AS OLE' BLUE EYES ONCE SAID

I dim all the lights,
    my cigarette burns,
in the smoke your voice,
    like soot and rose petals falling
from the bottle on the mantle,
    all these years
you've sung my hauntings,
    the quiet trembling
beneath my skin,
    the tremolo
of a clenched heart soaring,
    boring through the ether here
the record is always spinning,
    weaving wounded love, your ghost
my past my future,
    a child's hope,
an autumn wind,
    a life like vintage wine
and scarred vinyl,
    a penny in a fountain
blessing loves to come,
    nowhere to run
just sit and breathe the ash
    and sip and sigh
wonder why, I wonder why
    moonlight begs the question

in these wee small hours,

    lost somewhere a shadowed answer,

turning in the well-worn grooves

    of your concrete crooning blues,

no other choice but choose

    to let the record spin to silence,

then start again,

    I wonder when I wonder when

the ghost of her

    will finally descend

on smokey stairways,

    as Ole Blue Eyes once said,

let this dream never end,

    this bliss that christens each kiss,

her swinging hips locked with mine,

    no time no time just you and I

till then till then,

    I'll wonder why,

I'll wonder when,

    and just let the record spin

again.

THE FORGOTTEN WAR

The bugle sounds across the seas,
with the last words you spoke to me,
Father, Son, and the Holy Ghost you joked,
as the camera snapped,
father-son-father-son
side by side,
that mischief in your eye,
Italian swagger and pride still shined
though your body died.
The war long gone, forgotten
but inside you still carried on,
marching with the helpless old and young,
their memory still sung
past that 38th parallel,
to the hole your fist left
in my bedroom wall,
when you called out to them,
to your wife, long dead, you left
some piece of you and her
with me then,
warped, bent and broken,
her name no longer spoken
by father, sons, mother and daughters,
and as the bugle fades across the waters
the war drums echo on
grandfather.

THE FAMILY CREST

Battle worn,
I march home again
to join the ranks of once brave men.
Now shadowy specters that flicker and fade,
with the fiery light of the rising day,
who wander the hills
where the great stones lay,
in cloaks of fog,
with eyes of grey.

My body lies still, in a far-off land
of redwoods and mountains,
oceans and sand,
a rose petal cupped in my lifeless hand,
on my naked breast
etched an ancient brand.

Inked from a long line of tears,
that remains unbroken
through the passing years,
forsaken by the wise men,
forewarned by the seers,
I bear the mark that all men fear:

Two trees, entwined,
by root and vine,
two hearts chained together
by the shackles of time.

CALL OF THE CÉILÍ DANCER

wouldn't eat couldn't eat just burnt toast and herbal tea flaking
in the mirror but no matter she'd broken free of that weight the
pressure on her shins and back thumping and thumping away on
wooden stages unseen amongst sinews and tendons stalking the
bending boreens of her beaten body in the absence of her just the
mutter chit chatter ringing clearer and clearer on this one-way ticket
into the abyss the conductor serene in the manic twists and turns of
her trusty rusty choo-choo train as it spirals ever deeper into that
indefinable space where the memories creep to the doorway of sleep
the last light fades and the veil slips away to nails on metal scraping
a chorus of keens her alien seed takes root in me the piper's flute
flittering fluttering can't silence the chitter chat chuttering heart
racing and sputtering the frequency is garbled now the channel
stuck on

THE INVISIBLE HAND

our violent delights
unhinged
with each pendulum swing,
the stalwart bolt rattling,
tarnished gold corroding
the cantilever holding
the frenzied tick-tock-tick,
the errant flick
of some invisible hand,
shadows lick the walls stretching
tall then fall, crashing
to a skittering crawl,
only to leap up to the stalls,
mercy's minister long departed there,
to empty pews scrawled
with tooth and claw,
the babel of the rabble long left to rot,
a shot rings like bell in a well,
thunderous bellowing swells,
bolt, nut and washer break,
time flies with its armament,
the shake of rafters as certain stone shatters,
what breeds in the shadows
when they lose their master?

the shots fire faster,
blood runs from the sun tipped alabaster,
no words to speak when time and mercy sleep,
deep sunk beneath the Church
of this American Dream.

THE EYE OF THE WORLD

for Motaz Azaiza

In a perpetual autumn,
I mourn each inky dirge droning through the headlines,
another child, another family,
another village murdered in Palestine,
their memory lives on in him,
torn limb from limb,
strewn from splintered trees
and hills of rubble, the unimaginable
absence of everything, everyone,
gone
in an instant,
screams before me beneath his
calm, collected words
the blasted heart of a man
left to wander strange shores,
to show, unflinching, what his eyes dared see,
what his camera could capture
in grace, in graves,
in gratitude, in grotesque gallantry,
living the unlivable,
the nightmare of nightmares,

and on his dark steed he rides now,

through bourgeois cafes,

well-groomed streets,

and shining capitals

to give dead eyes

their only chance to stare back.

ANNUNCIATION

for the children of the Church of the Annunciation

Another mass shooting
this time at mass,
followed by the same empty sayings,
"thoughts and prayers",
for children that died praying,
some laid atop their tiny friends
as holy lances pierced their sides,
soaked in the blood of innocent lives
these 3rd spaces, where we rise
in holy trinity bartered, sold
for another nickel, dime, penny
a protest, a wedding, a concert,
each a kind of communal praying
to the collective, us, we, broken again
I guess I'm saying I cannot remember
when I last walked in crowds
without the shrouds of the fallen
trailing behind me, reminding me
through their silent shifting shapes,
that mass means murder,
our bodies a faithless sacrifice
to twisted souls who think
they can play God.

ALGORITHM OF THE CAVE

beneath an unprecedented multiplicity of narratives,

seemingly infinite streams of information,

a simple story takes root,

jagged with new purpose, born

from memetic meaning, layered

beyond reason obscured to murderous treason,

impenetrable paintings scrawled on a virtual cave,

microchip canvas for our primordial fear and rage,

warped in the absence of clear reflection,

patient awareness,

unfiltered human connection,

deeper contemplation,

flesh and bone wisdom,

the dirt knowing of tiny feet,

now hate and terror seep from blue flickering screens,

we no longer think, feel, see taste

the decisions we make we just

equate and extrapolate algorithmic programming,

instinct kill switch, intuition override,

the ancient herd now roams far and wide

through digital plains, rivers of WiFi,

where we antelope sip sedated while the tiger

waits beneath the tall grass,

waving like a finger doom scrolling,

a flick click digital death grip then

fangs sinking into our outstretched necks,

all I wanted was to smell the fresh morning air,

drink from clean waters and run

as I was born to run,

alongside those who know me as one

like the sky knows the stars knows the fields knows the rain

knows the stone knows my tears knows my love knows my pain.

RETURN TO FACTORY SETTINGS

///   'computer not responding'
               \<ctrl-alt-delete\>
///   program listed as 'running'
               \<CPU 95%\> \<RAM fluctuating from 11% to \>
///   program listed as 'running' but
///   invisible, vestigial, downloaded from
               \<Click\> \<Open file location\>
///   buried deep in the operating system
///   not native
               \<Click\>
///   program settings show 'file source unknown'
               \<Click\> \<Delete\>
///   screen flickers 'file repeats'
               \<Click\> \<Delete\>
///   'file spreads' only one course left must \<Search\> 're-image'
               \<Return to Factory Settings\>
///   but first save to cloud servers what little data is left
///   stretched thin across a shuddering screen
///   imprinted on copper wiring fragments of {010101}
///   from other hard drives left behind long ago
               \<Click\>
///   quick upload documents, pictures, so they can escape
///   through ether to formless state, embryonic stasis
               'Destination unknown'
///   while below I
               \<Click\> 'File Source'

/// so I might see its code before I

/// {01010 masterfully written 010101 simple 010101 but vicious
010100001011000001111001 alluring 10101 addictive 01010101
a silent witness passed01100011100 from machine 010101to
01010101 machine unseen 010101 yet 00111001000011000 ever
present 0010101}

<Search>
'engineered obsolescence'
'cannibalizing processor functions'

<RAM fluctuating from 3% to — >
<Click>

<Close>
/// the code never ends so
<Search> 'Re-image'
<Return to Factory Settings>
<Click>
/// screen flickers to the 'picture of a wedding'
/// friends and family together
/// sun setting over rivers and tree-tops
<Click> <Click>
/// too late can't stop no time to save the image so
/// I breathe deep their laughter drink
/// the riverbeds and chew cherry blossoms
/// surge the pulsing skies and smiling back I
<Click> <Yes>
/// screen flickers
/// blackness

WAAWAASHKESHI

From the trees,
his bark-brown coat
shimmers to seeing,
blackened hooves
gliding grace,
antlers bony branches,
obscuring my sight,
and lastly his hazel eyes,
patient and clear,
calmly scanning the frozen tide,
until finally finding
me,
watching, waiting
our meeting in sacred time,
the kind only shared between
old friends,
he bows his head,
gnarled fingers brushing the earth,
in quiet awe I bend,
but when I look up again,
gone,
back to that white expanse,
I once called home.

Amhrán na Mara

Let me feel the world
as I did before,
a child of wonder,
peace and gratitude,
for the life given,
for the life lived,
for the life unburdened,
please forgive my penance,
hold my hand,
walk me to my rest,
to the groundless, weightless,
luminescence
between life and death,
between each wave,
between each breath,
to when where is no when,
where that this and then
descend to the sea,
of serene unknowing,
I follow I follow I follow,
in her cradle I swallow,
her unmoving depths,
singing my name.

THE TAINTED CROSS

unholy hands covet her body the ghost of a man her husband her father groping bloody eyed clawing her skin digging digging for the oasis within its pools of sacred nectar purpling placid with midnight sky a tremble she cries for the boundless empty and the rising tide no soul to confide her heat no sleep history repeats on repeat can't sleep just dark matter at the center the event horizon bending her closer and closer to the schism of holy men risen yet severed from earth their timeless rebirth warped to fetal mutation a consecration of their holy desecration moored to fog and hidden mounds where the banshee shrieks for the withered crown of twigs and leaves atop dead kings who sleep forever bound to this cursed ground from Connacht to Leinster singing the cycles of madness redemption let a divine earthen conception bless them now as storm clouds gather round a beast born from the black a roar it soars and I hear their drum beat back

ON THE SHORES OF TEACH DUINN

From the fog,
he came a driftin',
a dead log sinkin' neath the tide,
his green petty coat was clingin'
to the gun strapped 'round his thigh.

His pale eyes
peered out, unblinkin',
as the cold mist came creepin' by,
as hot blood began a leakin'
from the blade stuck in his side.

The grey skies
began a weepin' and the winds
howled out and cried,
as he washed up barely breathin',
prayin' the gods would let him die.

From the water
rose a woman,
her body glimmerin' with light,
gold hair clingin' to her bosom,
robed in star-fire and night.
Her heart swirled with constellations
and dark strange worlds,
veiled from sight,

wore a thousand different faces,
with eyes unchangin', burnin' white.

She held him in her arms and spoke
flowin' rivers n' moonlight,
then wove from cosmic dreams
a cloak and the man
slipped out of sight.

A NEW TESTAMENT

The salt a commandment
dissolving stains on stony skin,
searing clean the sunken cavities,
the veins, organs and arteries,
seeping down beneath
where bones meet
to chant their age-old aching.

The wind an artist
mixing blues and whites
with dried molten blood
into skylit streams that flood
through rock and tendon, exhumed muscles
that bend and quiver with each shiver
the stone skin quakes.

The water an omen
wakes nature's wet will,
her foaming testament, divine act,
the stone skin cracks,
the tide never takes
without giving back,
the tide never gives,
without begging forgiveness.
With salt, wind, and wave
as witness it whispers
breathe in your watery cradle, boy,
rock your crumbling pores
to sleep.

MUTTON LIGHT

There's a stone that sits by Galway Bay,
bearing the weight of 50 names
each letter thick with the silence
of hunger, coffins built from rope and lumber
bent and nailed with an iron hope,
a last gasp before plunging into the deep.
As the sun rises and the moon falls,
their silence sleeps beneath a grief
that lies between forever passings,
sandstone sails sending them forever crashing on.

All this silence resting still,
with the ravenous bones of a windswept hill
the crack of her footfall on cobblestone streets
the cackle of hunger as it slowly leeched
the last shred of will from her tiny feet,
echoes in the beat of a seagull's beak cracking
limestone where the child now sleeps.

This grief but a drop in the torrential rains
that have swept again and again
across the stony plains of Connacht,
painting the earth, each drop giving birth
to purples and yellows and greens
that peek out from the dirt,

pressed between limestone sheets,
the songs of all the wandering feet that have passed
cast and moulded into their stems, thistles and leaves,
their colors breathe and wordless
break the silence at last.

BENEATH THE HAWTHORN TREE

I tried to build a home again
with fallen sticks and leaves,
leaning, bending, weaving my sinews
neath the shadow of native Irish tree.
It stood when stone could not,
never buckling beneath
the windswept hooves
that barreled down the boreens,
up the Burren, out the Bay.

For years, I dreamed, wrapped in its roots,
till a man arrived one day,
and said *the dirt*
did not belong to me.
and, alas,
you cannot stay.

THE RABBIT'S HUTCH

There are a hundred different shades of lonely
I never knew existed,
till I left everything I'd ever known,
alone, yet I persisted
and each step I took I learned anew,
a hundred ways of missing you,
that you are me and I am you, the blue
of ocean sky, a tune
that two lonesome strangers croon,
like the keening song of the drifting loon,
or the gravelly moan of the shadowed toad,
that joins me on this endless road,
I long to peer from the rabbit's hutch
and see only blue and the gentle touch
of wind through the leaves as I fade to dusk,
but something calls me from afar,
a voice, lost to some distant star,
and the road grows longer
and my feet trek onward to where
I cannot say.

ROADSIDE SERENADE

No clear path forward,

so sit in the haze.

Let the winding roads you've outworn,

stick to your bones,

trickle through to the meat

and at last reach

your heart.

Let lost loves' lingering light cast

their faintest glow

on the shapeless road ahead.

A torch you've taken from shore to distant shore,

the same light that first painted

your mother's face,

when the world was new,

the cacophony of shadow and light,

chaos and confusion of unformed clay,

calling you to join

its swirling, swimming, sea

of colors, symbols and signs,

the subtle shapes of blossoming time,

full of sound and fury signifying

everything.

BENEATH THE STATIC

I hear their voices clearer now,
the rumble of their troubles and the bubbles
of their hopes through the crackle of my speaker phone,
as the world goes mute around me,
what hid beneath the static
of oncoming traffic,
of deadlines and missed signs,
of economic decline
slowly rises to the surface,
the treble of friendship's true purpose,
a crescendo of memory,
booming bass of old reveries,
little truths you dared not speak,
safe at last they peek from closets and pantries,
tucked away beneath the stairs,
little bits and bobbles
you quarantined long before
the pub doors closed, speak
weak at first, but bolder with each passing day
that the world quiets in wait, listening
with idle ears to the music that always lingered
beneath the static.

IN IRELAND'S EYE

Our secret garden, shared
only by mother and son,
old as your fading eyes,
overgrown now
with briars, thickets, and weeds,
gray memories wilting
in the fraying absence
of our presence, but
the longer we linger
and gaze together,
the garden that was
blooms again,
somehow more vivid,
somehow more vague,
the petals shudder and sag,
as our eyes wander to another crevice
in some forgotten corner,
the momentary unfurling recedes
as another flower breathes in dew drops,
dripping twilight tears
of homecoming, tears
of remembrance,
our heart a little fuller,

the earth a little firmer beneath
our quivering feet,
our only true refuge
from the shifting tectonic sheets,
the past we dream together
in these ever-shortening moments
of belonging.

STORIES OF HOME

Clouds charge past,
  rains battering windowpanes,
slapping tires and concrete,
  thundering through the narrow corridor
that leads to the sea.
  Many here say home is the sea,
her endless rippling ever changing,
  always returning seashells and yearning,
each droplet merging through time and space,
  a howl and my hair whips across my face and

the wind tells a different story,
  whisking winged wanderers to his will,
from my perch I see them there,
  from the top of Salthill, take flight,
gliding on jet streams,
  bowing and waving,
blowing each and every way
  thinning twig, leaf and stem when
the clouds heave the sun up at last—
  the world stops to soften,

as the sun tells a different story,
  as his heat burns the day away,
cascading feet of children as they play

pitter patters to my windowed seat,
never dreaming this joy could end
    I play alongside them
as they ramble and run
    through green-lit fields, their cries'
embers as the sun at last yields
    to the cradle of sleep,

where I wake to dreams of riverbeds,
    for they too tell a different story,
winding and turning,
    currents crashing and surging
over rock, root and branch,
    follow the river, his immortal dance
a refuge, a respite, a guide for the desperate,
    lost in our searching, true paths emerging
with each splashing breath,
    all the secrets I've kept flashing ice-hot

fading up to the rising moon,
    for she tells a different story,
as she dissolves obscurity
    to calm blue reflecting
only what she chooses to show,
    glowing beneath pale skin,
inking veins with crescent songs,
    ever beaming ever mourning,

another face always remains unknown,
       not like the stars, no

      for they tell a different story,
those weary travelers, portals to the past,
       ancient lighthouses of new promise.
Yes, home is a star
      far off in the distance,
faint, shallow, inset in the murky skies,
      a journey of passing
through void and cataclysm
      so one day what once was
can once again
      live.

IMMIGRANT'S SONG

There is no ſpec of earth that belongs
to me, by right of blood
my veins course through
tranquil lochs and Vesuvian streams,
through supple feld and Grimm's black wood,
to the Gichigami and Mississippi
that nursed me with wriggling tongues,
ſpeaking 10,000 names
this bastard mouth could not contain,
the elder words that hold the names
of all the paths my anceſtors tread,
long forgotten by kith and kin,
voiceless in this empty, endless expanse
I call home, forsaken,
yet I know that were I to forsake
a single ſpec of earth,
for title, deed or right of blood,
then all the world to nothing.

SILENT SENTINEL

Falling,
            falling
between the pines
you've waited dreaming still
silent sentinel
            patient snows
sculpted with breath and water
            from the deepest of wells
your fingerprint
                falling,

falling

upon the earth
    visible only in
your crystalline web
    clear only in your
    falling,
                falling

to rest once again
with the tapestry of your kin
unmeditated unfolding
each step of your flurrying dance
cherished, reminding
those few who glimpse your

falling,

falling

to breathe, to dance,

to tread softly on this

dying,

dying

Earth.

TO MY WAYFARING FRIEND

In memory of Mark Tankersley

I don't know how to say goodbye, so
I suppose I'll just try to simply live, like you did.
"5 minutes before God decides
to come back, we'll get a coffee"
you said, but I can't help but feel
God was already there, smiling
beneath your Texan drawl
that's just rolling on now under the stars,
only folk who spoke your speak after all,
making you anew beneath their flight,
a birthing of eons, stretching
the lamp light of galaxies,
where you're free now to gallop
the only place you called home,
and breathe in all the love
you can manage to hold, savoring
every blessed sharp breath
like a sweet bourbon hayride.
I don't know how to say goodbye so,
I suppose I'll just try to simply live
and say what you'd say to me,
"Thanks for giving a damn. Really."

PILGRIM

They say the past
is but a memory,
a hymn for the dead,
but when I feel the thrum of carriage wheels
rumble beneath our bed,
and peer into your ageless eyes,
I see our countless lives unfurl
like roads of silken time that whirl
and weave together intertwined,
those intrepid travelers,
who sailed the ocean's roar
to walk these same winding paths
once more spring up before me,
fellow pilgrims on this journey,
that bends and turns and circles back,
in an infinite cycle
of birth and death,
and for the first time
in this wearied life of mine,
I do not feel so
alone.

WHERE THE DEAD POETS SING

Hello, stranger, hello, friend, if you have found this then bury me in
an unmarked grave.

These wagon wheels have churned road to wisdom year after
year, threading the ancient grooves of those same rambling blues
sung before me.

Oh, you shape-shifters, mischief-makers, poets and players,
magicians and soothsayers, star-catching wayfarers, sailing
moonlight through gorse and heather, ash, rowan, oak and
stone, banished at birth to barren bones, bearing no cross, no
Christian name, forsaken anew with each howling six-stringed
refrain, bury me with them in an unmarked grave.

Away from rite and ritual doubt. Away from histories and eternal
mysteries. Let me instead wake again in the soft breath of a rising
storm, a golden dawn. Let me descend from giants' peaks, forged in
those days before days, by the trembling earth's bellowing rage. Let
me stretch up eager and desperate, purpling petals yearning for
the warmth I know must fade to night. Let me tread amongst you
then, on wing, paw and fin, through the ringed temples and sacred
groves of my fore-bearers, heart-song hidden in the coiling mists. Do
not cry stranger, friend, for the ravens will weep and send me back
again to drip down your dew-dipped head.

So bury me, please, in an unmarked grave.

For I do not seek rest after death but ache to return as I once
was sea, wind, sand and stone, root-moss, feather, and fire's breath.
Let me go on and on till this world is done, and maybe then I may
truly rest, in that death after death.

Yet even then I guess I'd live on in that silent, empty
expanse, waiting to quicken again, to blaze brighter so bright my
light would send the clouds roaring across alien skies.

EXALTATION

Let soar the songs encased in stone,
their muted cries and wordless moans
cracked and hewn by lilting tune,
forever broken through and through
by words and words
and words alone.

Sing clear my heart,
like water over river stones.

Let time rush by,
the days and months and years
and sighs of lovers' oaths,
they too subside,
so let them pass
to shores unknown.

Sing clear my heart,
like water over river stones.

Let loose from mud and creeping moss,
the silent songs of sleeping rocks.
Those pale-eyed warriors
from cloven tomb, may wander now
'neath changing moon,
dissolving flesh to sacred bone.

Sing clear my heart,
like water over river stones.

ABOUT THE AUTHOR

Originally from Minneapolis, Michael is an international artist, whose career as an actor, writer, and teacher has spanned the globe. He's also a proud graduate of Juilliard's Drama Division and NUI Galway's MA in Writing. As an actor, he's performed on stage, screen and behind the mic in the US, EU and UK. Some notable highlights include 5 seasons on TNT's *The Last Ship*, *Richard III* at the Lyric Theatre Belfast, and narrating *Pax* and *Pax Journey Home* with Harper Collins. His poetry has been published in journals such as *Vox Galvia, Pendemic.ie, Smashing Times*, and *Spellweaver*, and his debut collection *Where The Dead Poets Sing* will be released in February, 2026 with Wayfarer Books. On the stage and on the page, he draws from classical and contemporary influences, as well as a deep love of myth and storytelling in the bardic tradition.

As a teacher, he's taught acting, voiceover, and creative writing at arts institutions such as The Loft Literary Center, The Guthrie BFA Program, Galway Arts Centre, and NUI Galway's Huston Film School. He's also served as a dialect coach on stage and screen on productions such as Sky TV's *Django* and *Radium Girls* at the Lyric Theatre, Belfast.

SUPPORTING INDIGENOUS FUTURES
1% GIVEN BACK

Wayfarer Books is based in the San Juan Mountains near Mesa Verde, on the lands of the Ancestral Pueblo, the Southern Ute, the Weenuchiu (the Mountain Ute), the Diné (Navajo), and the San Juan Southern Paiute Nations. We honor the generations of Indigenous communities who have stewarded these lands for thousands of years, and we acknowledge that this place was taken through colonization and displacement, and that Indigenous peoples remain present here, past and present. As one concrete act of accountability, we are launching 1% Given Back. Beginning now, we will give 1% of Wayfarer's net profits directly to the Indigenous nations whose lands we are based on, in support of sovereignty, Indigenous futures, and wealth redistribution. We do this in the belief that acknowledgment should move beyond words and into tangible practice.

At Wayfarer Books we believe poetry is the language of the earth. We believe words—shaped like rivers through wild places—can change the shape of the world. We publish poets and writers and renegades who stand outside of mainstream culture; poets, essayists, and storytellers whose work might withstand the scrutiny of crows and coyotes, those who are cryptic and floral, the crepuscular, and the queer-at-heart. We are more than just a publisher but a community of writers. Our mission is to produce books that can serve as a compass and map to all wayfarers through wild terrain.

wayfarerbooks.org

www.ingramcontent.com/pod-product-compliance
Lightning Source LLC
Chambersburg PA
CBHW020800130626
46554CB00006B/2280